# Introduction

**A**dvent is a season almost forgotten by the secular world. You'll find Advent calendars, but they are simply an adornment for the "Christmas season," which begins sometime after Halloween and ends on Christmas day.

This booklet is designed to help you and your family capture some of what's intended by the liturgical season of Advent. Each day has a Scripture quote, a brief reflection, and an action to complete.

What I hope you gain from this booklet is an appreciation of Advent. Do as much—or as little—as you can each day. It is not as important to do every reflection and activity as it is for you and your family to enjoy the anticipation of Christ's birth.

Everyone will enjoy this time more if it doesn't become just one more thing added to an already busy time of year. Try to find a quiet moment each day and spend it together. Don't try to read or plan ahead; just embrace each day as the page turns.

You'll notice the book continues a bit *after* Christmas day, and that's because the Christmas season properly *begins* on December 25 and lasts, in the Church's calendar, until the feast of the Baptism of the Lord. After all your presents have been opened and the decorations put away, we still have a Baby who changed the world and who is, at the heart of it, the biggest reason for our celebration. Everything else is secondary to the arrival of our Messiah.

May your Advent be blessed this year, and may your Christmas be better for the preparation you do during Advent.

—Sarah Reinhard

# Get Ready

*Watch, therefore; you do not know when the lord of the house is coming, whether in the evening, or at midnight, or at cockcrow, or in the morning.*

**MARK 13:35**

## Think

What would you do if a king were coming to visit you? You'd want to know ahead of time that he was coming, wouldn't you? You would probably want to straighten up a few things and find ways to make your house special for the king's arrival.

Each year, a King does come to us. He comes as a baby, in a small trough in a rough cave. Though his place in time was thousands of years ago, we are invited to meet him again every year as though for the first time.

Christmas seems so far away on this first Sunday of Advent. The Christmas decorations have not been put up in the church, though an Advent wreath is probably in place.

The stores, however, are decorated and blaring Christmas music. It's enough to make us think it's the Christmas season, but it's not. Not until December 25.

During this time of waiting, we have a lot to do. We might have presents to buy and decorations to hang, but there are even more important things. We have to make sure we are ready.

Sometimes all the other things about Christmas distract

4

## Light a Candle

# The HOPE candle

us from the real event, the birth of the Christ Child. Sometimes we forget about the real story that started it all.

This week, we'll focus on getting ready for Christmas. One way we can do that is to ask Jesus to help us every day. Every year, we have a chance to meet him again in the manger, and every year, we have a season to help us get ready. Let's spend our Advent turning to Jesus with every little part of our day.

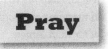

**Pray**

*Jesus, help me get ready for your birth. Help me to see past the shiny decorations in all the stores and to remember that I'm waiting for you. Amen.*

**Act**

**One way to get ready for Jesus is to make an Advent resolution. What can you give Jesus? Is there a person you can be nice to all during Advent? Could you help someone in a special way during Advent? Think of something you can do to get ready for Jesus' birth.**

As we light the first purple candle, we can think of the hope we have in the coming of the Lord. Remember the angel's visit to Mary, the visit at the Annunciation that got things started. We walk with Mary this week as we get ready with her for the coming of our Savior.

# Monday
## First Week of Advent

**Think**

When you get ready to go somewhere important, you probably make sure that you look nice and that you have the things you need.

Advent is no different. We are getting ready for a day that changes the world again and again: Christmas.

No one expected the Messiah to come as a simple baby, a human just like us, who suffered and who even died.

No one will expect him when he comes again at the end of time. We are reminded throughout this first week of our Advent journey that we always have to be ready. We have to have our lives in order, from the biggest to the smallest of things. We don't want to disappoint our King!

**Pray**

*Jesus, thank you for the gift of Advent, for the chance to get ready for Christmas. Help me to remember you in the midst of all the things going on around me. Give me the strength to turn to you for help. Amen.*

**Act**

**As you think about the way you'll get your heart ready, clean and pick up toys in a room in your house.**

Get Ready

# Tuesday
## First Week of Advent

As we prepare for our Messiah to come, we should be examining our lives and our hearts. Do we act the way we should? Are we treating people with respect and love? Is there an area in our lives that needs special attention during this season of Advent preparation?

Let's think of our heart as a house that King Jesus will be coming to visit. We want it to be clean and neat, ready for him. We should sweep it free of all the grudges we hold against other people. We should be mindful of how we treat the people around us, especially those closest to us, the ones we see every day. We should also think of the things Jesus has asked us to do in the Ten Commandments, especially honoring our parents.

Advent is a time each year to realize we are awaiting a grand guest. He will be just a baby, one who is totally dependent on us, but we have to be ready for the gift of his visit. He is trusting us to take care of him, and we want to do that to the best of our ability.

*Therefore, stay awake! For you do not know on which day your Lord will come.*
MATTHEW 24:42

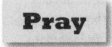

*Jesus, help me to see the areas in my life that I need to work on before you come on Christmas day. Give me the grace to change the one small thing that will be a gift to you. Amen.*

**Today, think of one way you can get ready for Jesus. Maybe you can help your mom around the house. Maybe you need to make up with someone who has hurt you or whom you have hurt. Whatever it is, remember that Jesus will help you.**

GetReady

May he not
come suddenly
and find you
sleeping.

MARK 13:36

# Wednesday
## First Week of Advent

**Think** Sleep is a necessary part of our lives. Sometimes when we don't get enough sleep, it shows in our actions.

Though sleep is necessary, it's also used, especially in the Gospel readings for the first week of Advent, as a symbol of laziness. This week, we're trying to get ready for Jesus' coming. We don't want to be caught sleeping.

Have you ever overslept and missed something important? How does it feel when you wake up late and have to rush around getting ready to leave?

We don't want Christmas day to come as a surprise, the kind that leaves us frazzled and stressed. We want it to be an experience of joy and love for our Savior. His coming is a gift, after all.

To be ready, though, we have to do our work now. We have to forgive the people who have hurt us and let go of any pain from our past. It isn't easy, but Jesus will help us in this important work.

**Pray** *Jesus, I want to be ready for you on Christmas day. Help me to be awake for your coming, and help me to forgive the people who have hurt me today. Amen.*

**Act** **Before bedtime, kneel and say a prayer—perhaps an Our Father, Hail Mary, and Glory Be—for a person who annoyed you today. Get your heart ready by offering this gift for them.**

GetReady

# Thursday

## First Week of Advent

### Think

With today's Scripture, we have the image of loudness. If you have never heard the roar of ocean waves, think of a loud piece of machinery or an explosion of thunder. Loud noises get our attention.

Christmas day is a sort of loud noise waiting to happen, but it doesn't happen with a bang. It happens in the silence of a stable, in the middle of a small town, with only a few witnesses.

Shouldn't the Son of God have come with a big bang? That's what everyone expected, but it's not what happened. God doesn't often operate with loud noises or flashes of lightning. God gets our attention in small ways, using the silence of our hearts.

Before we can hear the still, small voice of the Holy Spirit, though, we need silence. As we prepare this week, let's try to find some quiet time in our day to spend with God, talking with him and listening for him.

### Pray

*Jesus, so often my life is loud and filled with busy-ness. Help me to be still and quiet, waiting for you to come. Amen.*

### Act

**Use a soft voice today. Be extra-patient with the people around you, especially the ones who usually get on your nerves or frustrate you.**

*There will be signs in the sun, the moon, and the stars, and on earth nations will be in dismay, perplexed by the roaring of the sea and the waves.*
LUKE 21:25

Get Ready

# Friday
## First Week of Advent

*So too, you also must be prepared, for at an hour you do not expect, the Son of Man will come.*
MATTHEW 24:44

**Think** How do you feel when something happens that you weren't expecting? Do you like to be surprised? What if it's not a surprise you like?

We're told Jesus will come at an unexpected time. Chances are, we'll have other plans and other things to do.

Is Christmas a time when you envision getting presents? Is it a time for getting up early and eating a special meal? What if it doesn't turn out the way you want?

Preparing ourselves means being open to what God has in mind instead of limiting ourselves to what we want. God knows what's best for us, and he will help us deal with the circumstances we have to face in life.

This isn't just about Christmas day; it's about our lives. Advent is a time to get ready for Jesus' birth, but it's also a time of grace when we can give Baby Jesus the gift of changing our inner selves. We can become nicer during Advent and stay nicer once it's over.

To be ready for Jesus, we have to keep working on ourselves.

**Pray** *Jesus, though Christmas is still a long way off, I want to be ready. Give me the strength to change myself to be more prepared for your coming. Help me to see that when I give of myself, I receive the greatest blessing in being more like you. Amen.*

**Act** Help in the kitchen today without being asked. Set the table or clear it after a meal, do the dishes or empty the dishwasher, or find another way to help.

Get Ready

# Saturday
## First Week of Advent

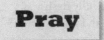

This time of year, there are always a lot of parties and great food. You'll find cookies and candies wherever you go, and maybe you'll even have the chance to eat as much as you want.

There's also pressure at this time of year—maybe you don't feel it, but you might sense it in the people around you. There seems to be so much to do that if we're not careful, we might forget what we're preparing for.

Today's Scripture reminds us that we are supposed to be ready for Christmas. More than a day on the calendar, we are to experience it in our hearts.

The birth of Jesus changed the world, and it continues to change it. He's coming to visit us, and we want to be waiting with a smile on our face. The time to celebrate is not yet here. We're still getting ready.

*Jesus, I want to be ready when you come, but there are so many distractions. Everyone's acting like it's already Christmas! Help me to get ready for you. Amen.*

**Give up one thing today, whether a favorite food or an activity. Discover how giving up something you like will help you get ready for the great feast of Christmas.**

*Beware that your hearts do not become drowsy from carousing and drunkenness and the anxieties of daily life, and that day catch you by surprise like a trap. For that day will assault everyone who lives on the face of the earth.*
LUKE 21:34–35

Get Ready

11

# Repent

*In those days John the Baptist appeared, preaching in the desert of Judea [and] saying, "Repent, for the kingdom of heaven is at hand!"*

**MATTHEW 3:1–2**

## Think

We are a week closer to Christmas, and you can probably tell by looking around. Have you started shopping for gifts? Does it seem like Christmas will never come? Are you getting excited?

Part of our Advent focus is repentance, and in today's Gospel, we hear John the Baptist loudly proclaim, "Repent, for the kingdom of heaven is at hand!" But what does that mean?

Jesus brings the kingdom to Earth when he becomes human. He is completely divine and completely human—fully God and fully flesh and blood. He's like us and yet very much not like us.

We started last week by getting ready. This week we will continue to prepare our hearts, focusing on repentance. That doesn't mean we have to beat ourselves up or feel undue guilt. Ridding ourselves of the burden of guilt and making things right with the people around us—and maybe even establishing some new habits—will open us further to the experience of the manger,

# the peace candle

the glory of Christmas, and the King who awaits us as a little baby.

Part of our excitement for Christmas can come from the lightness we are sure to feel when we repent fully. In what ways do we sin over and over? How do we resist what's best for us, what God wants for us, what we should do? When can we make time to fix these faults?

This week, as we focus on repentance, consider saying a special prayer to the Holy Spirit, asking for guidance. Ask him to help you listen—not to the loud Christmas noise, but to God's still, small voice.

*Jesus, guide me to see the ways I need to repent to be ready for you this Christmas. Amen.*

**Act**

**How are you doing with your Advent resolution? Promise yourself to continue working** on it this week, and ask Baby Jesus to help you when you struggle.

Lighting the second purple candle, we can think about the peace that comes from repentance. Making things right with the people in our lives frees us from the burdens that can get in the way of our embrace of the Savior. Our journey this week is bringing us closer to the peace that surpasses all understanding, that of Jesus.

*People of the whole Judean countryside and all the inhabitants of Jerusalem were going out to him and were being baptized by him in the Jordan River as they acknowledged their sins.*

MARK 1:5

Repent

# Monday

## Second Week of Advent

**Think**

It's hard to admit when we do something wrong. However, admitting when we've done wrong or when we have hurt someone else can be very healing for us, even if it makes us feel uncomfortable. Knowing we can be friends again is comforting.

Our family insists that the person who has been wronged must say "I forgive you" to the person saying "I'm sorry." It is consoling when those you have hurt—whether you meant to or not—say they forgive you.

God does that for each of us in our baptism. People must have been going to the Jordan River to experience baptism with John the Baptist because it feels so good to be forgiven.

Imagine yourself covered in dirt and grime and sweat. Then you take a hot bath, and when you come out wrapped in a towel, you are clean. Baptism does that for us, and so does confession.

When we tell God we are sorry, he replies, "I forgive you." In those three words, we can hear three other words, "I love you."

Repentance is an act of love. We show God we love him by apologizing—to him and to those we have wronged. He responds by hugging us tightly and forgiving us. Let's try to be just as generous with our forgiving too.

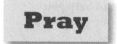

*Jesus, I know I have wronged some people. Help me to have the courage to tell them I'm sorry. Help me, also, to forgive those who apologize to me, both with my words and in my heart. Amen.*

**Obey the first time you're asked to do anything today, all day long. Your obedience will be a way of avoiding the need to repent or apologize later.**

# Tuesday
## Second Week of Advent

**Think** Repentance and forgiveness go hand-in-hand. We say we're sorry, and we are forgiven.

It sounds so easy, but often it's not. What if the other person doesn't really forgive us and holds a grudge? What if we are so hurt we have a hard time forgiving? What if we don't really think we should have to apologize?

Christmas is getting closer. Have we made our peace with those around us? Are we acting in a way that wouldn't embarrass us if God were to show up in person? Do we treat the people in our lives like the gifts they are?

We can see God in the people around us, from our parents to our siblings to our friends. The most difficult and annoying people are still children of God, and we are to treat them as Jesus would. That means that even if we've been hurt by them, we need to forgive them.

We can't be forgiven if we don't ask. We have to say we're sorry—we have to repent. It can seem like a lot of work, but God will help us. We just have to pray for his help.

**Pray** *Jesus, I want to repent. Help me to see where I need to improve and how you can help me. Amen.*

**Act** **Admit to being wrong and say "I'm sorry" today. If you have the opportunity, forgive someone who apologizes to you.**

*He went throughout [the] whole region of the Jordan, proclaiming a baptism of repentance for the forgiveness of sins.*
**LUKE 3:3**

Repent

# Wednesday
## Second Week of Advent

*I have baptized you with water; he will baptize you with the holy Spirit.*

**MARK 1:8**

**Think**

Water is one of the symbols of the Holy Spirit, and it calls to mind our baptism. We are baptized with water, and God washes away our sins. At confirmation, we receive the gift of the Holy Spirit, though you can still call on the Holy Spirit even if you have not been confirmed.

When John the Baptist baptized people, he could only use regular water. The sacrament of baptism was not in use yet and couldn't be experienced in the way we know it until the Holy Spirit came at Pentecost, the beginning of the Church.

John's baptism was refreshing to people; they were healed by being able to repent of their sins and experience God's forgiveness. It might seem strange to spend time thinking about repentance at this time of year. Your Christmas tree might be standing and lit, and you might have already celebrated Christmas parties or exchanged gifts.

Even so, we are still waiting for the Baby to come. We need to keep looking within ourselves and acting the way we know Jesus wants us to act. The Holy Spirit will help us with this.

**Pray**

*Jesus, I want Christmas to be here. I'm so excited! Help me to remember to act kindly and to be truly sorry and forgiving to everyone in my life. Amen.*

**Act**

**Say a prayer to the Holy Spirit before bedtime tonight.**

*Repent*

# Thursday
## Second Week of Advent

 **Think** Being sorry is more than just saying the words. We have to show we're sorry with our actions. It's especially important that we remember what we have done and try not to repeat it.

In confession, we are given a penance after we're forgiven. This isn't because God needs us to do anything extra. He knows the state of our heart. The penance is a way of helping us to remember and avoid that sin in the future.

In today's Gospel, John the Baptist tells us to "produce good fruit as evidence of your repentance." One way we can produce good fruit is to do nice things for people, even when they don't ask us to or they're not expecting it. We can pray for those who annoy us, be extra nice to those who frustrate us, and forgive those who continue to wrong us.

Being humble and aware of our own failings is hard. We can practice this by thinking about our actions at the end of each day and then praying an Act of Contrition. Whom did we hurt? Did we disobey anyone? Did we break any of the Ten Commandments?

Producing "good fruit" can be as simple as picking up our room or making our bed. It can be setting the table or helping a sibling. Let's work on our "good fruit" today so that when Jesus comes on Christmas day, we have a great gift to give him.

*When he saw many of the Pharisees and Sadducees coming to his baptism, he said to them, "You brood of vipers! Who warned you to flee from the coming wrath? Produce good fruit as evidence of your repentance."*
MATTHEW 3:7–8

 **Pray** *Jesus, I want to give you "good fruit" in my words and deeds. Help me to see what I can do and how I can be of service. Amen.*

**Act** **Reflect on the day and fix something you have broken, whether it's someone's feelings or an object.**

Repent

*Every valley
shall be filled
and every
mountain and
hill shall be
made low.
The winding
roads shall be
made straight,
and the rough
ways made
smooth,
and all flesh
shall see the
salvation of
God.*

LUKE 3:5–6

Repent

# Friday
## Second Week of Advent

**Think**

In the midst of our week focusing on repentance, we're given a hopeful image. Can you picture it? How does it make you feel?

Repentance isn't easy. We know that. Knowing we can be forgiven—quickly and completely—should fill us with hope.

More than anything else, Advent is a season of hope. As we prepare for Christ's coming at Christmas, we should see the great gifts that surround us. What are the blessings that make you smile today? What are you thankful for?

Have you ever apologized for something you thought would get you in big trouble, only to have the person hug you and tell you it was no big deal? How did that make you feel? What lesson did you learn?

There is hope for us. There is always hope: Advent is a season to remind us of this. Let's spend the day thanking God for the gift of hope.

**Pray**

*Jesus, I'm so glad you came as a baby. So often, I don't think of you as a child like I am. Show me how to remain hopeful even when I am filled with sadness or disappointment. Amen.*

**Act**

**Draw or find a picture that makes you feel hopeful. Hang it where you can see it, and every time you do, thank God for the blessings in your life.**

# Saturday
## Second Week of Advent

**Think** John the Baptist is often used as an example of humility. As a very powerful prophet in his time, he could have taken credit for a lot of things. When asked, though, he always admitted he was not the Messiah; in fact, he said the One who was coming after him was so great that John was not worthy to touch his sandals.

He's not just pretending Jesus is more important; he really knows it. Being humble is about accepting who we are and the role we have. We have to obey our parents and those in authority. We owe it to the people around us to always treat them with respect and charity.

Sometimes it's easier to be nice to the people who don't live with us than it is to be nice to the people who are closest to us. Our family and those who are around us all the time seem to be able to irritate us faster than anyone else. They see a side of us that usually only comes out when we are at home, totally relaxed.

Let's remember we owe it to these people to be mindful of our role—to love and support—and aware of how we treat them.

*And this is what he proclaimed: "One mightier than I is coming after me. I am not worthy to stoop and loosen the thongs of his sandals."*
**MARK 1:7**

**Pray** *Jesus, I get so annoyed with my family sometimes. They know just what to do to make me angry. Please give me the strength to be gentle and loving, even when I am feeling frustrated. Amen.*

**Act** **Say you're sorry and ask for forgiveness from someone in your family whom you've wronged.**

Repent

# Love

> Jesus said to them in reply, "Go and tell John what you hear and see: the blind regain their sight, the lame walk, lepers are cleansed, the deaf hear, the dead are raised, and the poor have the good news proclaimed to them."
>
> **MATTHEW 11:4–5**

## Think

In the picture of the Son of God as a human being, we see proof of God's love for us. Why else would he choose to come to Earth, to face the challenges we face, to suffer as we do?

But God doesn't stop just with sending his Son as a baby who has to grow up just like everyone else. When Jesus begins his ministry, he performs many miracles. Today's words from the Gospel of Matthew give us examples of the healings he does. They are physical examples; what we don't hear about today are the many ways in which Jesus heals people internally, within their souls.

We are hurt in many ways throughout our lives. We fall and scrape our knees, maybe even break a bone, but we also have our feelings hurt. These things happen to us many times, sometimes on a daily basis.

After a while, it can make us sad, tired, ready to drop. It becomes easy to forget

# The JOY candle

that God loves us, especially when we find ourselves wrapped in pain.

On Christmas day, we see God's love for us in a tiny Baby, huddled in a barn with his parents and some animals. He was born among the poorest of the poor, and yet he would save the world from its sin.

Our goal this week is to show Jesus we love him and to share Jesus' love with those around us. We want to be the gentle helper, the soothing friend, the patient worker.

We can show Jesus we love him in many different ways. The first and most important place we need to concentrate on is in our own families, with the people we see every single day.

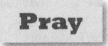

*Jesus, I love you and want to be like you in my words and deeds. Help me this week to show love to the people around me. Amen.*

**Advent will be over soon. Are you still working on your Advent resolution? Don't give up! Jesus will give you the help you need to make it to Christmas day.**

The pink candle reminds us that even though Advent is a penitential season, joy is all around us. As we journey through Advent, we empty ourselves of the extra and unneeded, opening ourselves to be filled by Jesus. This week as we practice love, let's feel the joy of the season.

# Monday
## Third Week of Advent

Jesus gives John the Baptist a very high compliment in today's quote from Scripture by saying that none are greater, but there seems to be a contradiction when Jesus says the least in the kingdom of heaven are greater than John. What does this mean?

Jesus is reminding everyone how important it is to be small and humble. This does not mean that we do not stand up for ourselves when we are mistreated. It means, instead, that we do not forget that God is first and that his will should determine how we live our lives. John the Baptist never tooted his own horn; he always gave God all the credit.

We are all called to be like the least in the kingdom of heaven; God wants us to serve those around us, to help the poor and feed the hungry. Some people are called to be rich and famous, and there is a lot of responsibility in that. Our goal should be to try to follow God's will for our lives, to love him enough to say "Yes" to what he is asking from us right here, right now.

Maybe we have a bed that needs to be made, an assignment that should be finished, a friend who could use a hug. There are many ways to show love in our everyday lives, and when we are generous with our love, we not only show God to those around us, but we find him in the people we meet.

*Amen, I say to you, among those born of women there has been none greater than John the Baptist; yet the least in the kingdom of heaven is greater than he.*
MATTHEW 11:11

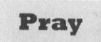

*Jesus, it's hard to show love to other people when I have so much else to do. Guide me in my day-to-day activities so that I show your love to other people. Amen.*

**It's easy to forget that we should always be looking for the good in other people, especially those we're around every day. Tell every member of your family one thing you appreciate about them.**

Love

# Tuesday
## Third Week of Advent

 In many parts of the world, Advent is a time of darkness. The days get shorter in December, and the nights get longer. Even during the daytime, it's often cold and cloudy.

The dark and cold can remind us of the loneliness many people experience at this time of year. Maybe they miss a loved one or are far from their family; maybe they are sick and in physical pain; maybe they are having other troubles.

How can we help these people? How do we know who they are? Can you think of someone who could use a kind word, a hug, or a special card?

We continue to prepare our hearts during this Advent season. The more love we show to those around us, the more we will find ourselves open to seeing God's love.

*He came for testimony, to testify to the light, so that all might believe through him.*

**JOHN 1:7**

 *Jesus, I know that many people around me are hurting at this time. Let me be of service to them and show them your love. Amen.*

 **At each meal today, pray for someone who lives far away. Send a special card or gift to let them know you are praying for them.**

*Love*

# Wednesday
## Third Week of Advent

**Think**

Helping others can be very rewarding. It can also be a lot of work and very inconvenient. It's easy to give away things we don't want, but what about sharing the things we like?

There is a lot of need in the world, though many of us don't see it up close in our daily lives. Many people have no home to live in, no food to eat, and are wearing the only clothes they own. We think of faraway places like Africa, but these people live in the city right down the road, and some of them might be people you know.

Today's Scripture mentions sharing clothing and food, which are two things everyone needs. What if you did not have clothes to wear tomorrow? What would you do if there was nothing in the cupboard for dinner tonight? How would you feel if someone came and brought you not just any clothes and food, but the very best?

That's what Jesus does for each of us when he comes on Christmas day: he brings us the very best. He shows us that being poor is not something we should fear, but something that paves the way for others to help.

It is our responsibility to help those who have less than we do. Even children can do this, if only through daily prayers and little sacrifices made for those who have greater needs than our own.

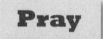

**Pray**

*Jesus, I know there are many people who have less than I do. I want to help, but I'm only a kid. Show me the way to share your love by sharing what I have. Amen.*

**Act**

**Do something for someone who has less than you, whether it's donating clothing or toys, saving your allowance to buy canned goods for the food pantry, or something else.**

*He said to them in reply, "Whoever has two tunics should share with the person who has none. And whoever has food should do likewise."*

LUKE 3:11

*Love*

# Thursday
## Third Week of Advent

**Think**

Sometimes it's easy to take the people we see all the time for granted. We forget that our parents work hard to make our lives comfortable. We don't think about the sacrifices our teachers make for us. We show up at church events and never consider the planning that went into them.

At this point in Advent, it's also easy to forget we're not in the Christmas season—not yet. It's so close. We can count the days and see it coming closer on the calendar. We might be done shopping and wrapping, and we might have our decorations up around the house.

Jesus is coming, but he's still not here. Though the presents taunt us and the anticipation is growing, we still have some final work to do to prepare ourselves.

Who are the people in your life who do the most for you? Have you thanked them? Have you told them you love them? Have you shown them you love them?

*John answered them, "I baptize with water; but there is one among you whom you do not recognize, the one who is coming after me, whose sandal strap I am not worthy to untie."*
JOHN 1:26–27

**Pray**

*Jesus, I know Christmas is close, and I'm so excited! I want it to be here. Help me to remember to keep showing love to the people around me, even though I'm getting impatient for the big day. Amen.*

**Act**

**Consider those who do a lot for you and whom you might take for granted. Write a thank-you card to three of these people in your life.**

Love

# Friday
## Third Week of Advent

**Think** John the Baptist never tries to be who he isn't. He's up-front with the Jews and tells them, "I am not the Messiah."

It must have confused them a bit because he was doing things no prophet had ever done before and saying things no one had ever said.

Sometimes we forget who we are and what we're supposed to be doing. We think what we want is more important than our duties; we ignore our responsibilities and pursue fleeting pleasures. Instead of praying, we play. Instead of obeying, we hide. Instead of speaking up for someone who needs us, we stay quiet.

John's example in today's Scripture can remind us how we should act. We should always point others to God, though we usually don't have to use words to do that. Our actions speak loudly about what we believe and what's important to us.

And the most important people we can impact are the ones we see every single day.

**Pray** *Jesus, I'm sorry for the times I have ignored you. It's so easy to get distracted by all the other things in my life. Guide me as I try to show your love to the people around me. Amen.*

**Act** **Complete a task around the house as a surprise for your parents.**

And this is the testimony of John. When the Jews from Jerusalem sent priests and Levites [to him] to ask him, "Who are you?" he admitted and did not deny it, but admitted, "I am not the Messiah."

JOHN 1:19–20

*Love*

# Saturday
## Third Week of Advent

 Today's quote from Scripture refers to farming in a way that would have been familiar to the people in Jesus' time but might not make any sense to us. Wheat grows with a protective covering over its seed. The seed is what we harvest and want to use, which we usually just call "wheat." The "chaff" is the part we don't want.

Farmers now use combines and machinery that automatically separate the wheat and chaff, keeping the wheat for food purposes and throwing the chaff back into the field. Two thousand years ago this was done by hand, using a winnowing fan. The chaff was often burned or otherwise discarded.

We want to be the wheat; we want to be valuable and sinless in God's sight. We want to be gathered into his barn, used for his purposes, giving him glory. To do this, we have to remember the purpose of our Advent journey: to prepare for the coming of Christ.

As we finish our week, we should not forget our call as Christians to show love to the people around us at all times. As Advent ends and we draw closer to Christmas, we should not relax our efforts to be loving and kind and generous with the people in our lives.

 *Jesus, I want to be with you, but I know that I often fail. Give me the courage to ask for forgiveness and show love just as you do. Help me to be the wheat and throw away the chaff in my life. Amen.*

 **Make a special gift for someone who's lonely during the holiday season.**

*His winnowing fan is in his hand to clear his threshing floor and to gather the wheat into his barn, but the chaff he will burn with unquenchable fire.*

LUKE 3:17

Love

# Anticipate

> *And coming to her, he said, "Hail, favored one! The Lord is with you."*
>
> **LUKE 1:28**

## Think

Christmas is so close, it's hard to remember we're still in Advent. Our anticipation is at a high point.

Anticipation is more than excitement. It's a matter of taking action so that we are prepared. We have spent the last three weeks focusing on getting ready, repenting, and loving. This week, we want to make sure we are anticipating—not just waiting passively, but actively searching for Christ in our daily lives.

Where can we find Jesus? How can we *be* Jesus? What do we still have to do to make our hearts and minds ready for his coming?

This is the most important gift we give all year: the gift of ourselves to the Christ Child.

Today's verse reminds us of an important helper we have—his mother, Mary. When the angel Gabriel greeted Mary, he used a phrase that's only been used for Mary: "favored one," or "full of grace."

Grace is what we need to get through this last week and to be ready for Baby Jesus.

## the LOVE candle

Mary can help us to be open to the grace God is trying to give us; she will help us say yes to God, just like she did.

Maybe it will be in our attitude. Maybe it will be in how we treat other people. Maybe there's someone we need to make peace with.

This week, as we wait in joyful anticipation, let's ask Mary to lead us to her Son, to the manger where we'll find the answer to all our needs.

**Pray** *Jesus, we're so close. Help me remember that I have important work to do before we reach Christmas, and help me remember to ask your mother for help when I need it. Amen.*

**Act** **This is the last week of Advent: how is it going with your Advent resolution? If you are struggling, remember to ask Jesus, Mary, and your guardian angel to help you make it to Christmas day.**

We're so close! The last purple candle might not even have a chance to burn for more than a couple of days. As we anticipate Christmas, let's feel the love even deeper that this special birth means for us. God loved us so much he sent his Son, and he sends him again every single year. Light this candle and know the love of God.

# Monday

## Fourth Week of Advent

*Then the angel
said to her,
"Do not be
afraid, Mary,
for you have
found favor
with God."*

LUKE 1:30

**Think** Why would Mary, who had no sin, be afraid of an angel? What did she do to find favor with God? How can we turn to her and follow her example?

As we wait eagerly—and maybe a little impatiently—for Christmas day, the Gospels point us to Mary. It's a good time to consider Jesus' mom. She was a very special woman and remains very involved in the lives of all of us, her children here on Earth.

Angels are not the little winged babies we sometimes see in pictures; they are powerful spirits that fight for God. The fact that Mary was afraid tells us something about how we can rely on our guardian angels, the ones God has given us to protect us.

Mary's example can inspire us and teach us how to approach God. She probably spent a lot of time in prayer, even though she was a busy housewife and mother. We can pray even while we're busy doing other things, and we can always ask Mary—and our guardian angel—to help us in our prayers.

**Pray** *Jesus, sometimes it's hard to picture your mother—or you, for that matter—as people I can approach. It's easy to forget you love me more than anyone else. Teach me to recognize your love in my life. Amen.*

**Act** Before going to bed, give God one of your biggest fears. Ask him to take it, and ask your guardian angel to pray for you to be freed from it.

*Anticipate*

# Tuesday
## Fourth Week of Advent

 **Think**
When Mary calls herself "the handmaid of the Lord," she's saying she's God's servant. It's hard for us to relate to the idea of servants in our modern world. Most of us do our own dishes and laundry and most of the other work around the house. We don't really live in a world with a lot of servants, at least not in the sense Mary was referring to in this passage.

When we are asked to do work we might consider "servant" work, how do we respond? Are we happy to have the chance to help someone? Do we look at our joyful completion of that work as a gift we give to God?

Mary teaches us an important lesson today and reminds us that we should always serve others in every part of our lives. We might just be making our bed or picking up the socks left in the living room, but we can make a big difference with the little things we do throughout our days.

Let's try to be like Mary this week as we wait for Christmas day. Let's use the energy we feel from being excited to serve someone else, someone who hasn't asked us but who we know needs us.

*Mary said, "Behold, I am the handmaid of the Lord. May it be done to me according to your word." Then the angel departed from her.*
LUKE 1:38

 **Pray**
*Jesus, I don't always like serving others. It's not always fun, and I have other things I want to do. Give me the desire to serve this week in anticipation of the gift of yourself that you will bring to all of us on Christmas day.*

 **Act**
**Write down one thing you can do to serve others. Post it where you will see it every day this week.**

*Anticipate*

# Wednesday
## Fourth Week of Advent

**Think**

We sin in many small ways each and every day. Those sins add up, and they can make it easier to commit bigger and bigger sins. That's why we should always be conscious of our actions and of what God wants us to do.

Jesus comes on Christmas day to save us from our sins. He wants to help us and make us more like him. He can only do that, though, if we cooperate with him.

The gift of the Christ Child is often turned down. Many times, we don't want to change how we act to receive the gift of the Baby Jesus.

What do we need to change? There's still time. There's always hope.

**Pray**

*Jesus, it's hard to change how I act, but I want to be ready for you. Give me the guidance and dedication to become more like you. Amen.*

**Act**

**Examine your conscience, and pray the Act of Contrition. If you can, go to confession.**

Anticipate

# Thursday
## Fourth Week of Advent

 Do you ever struggle when you have to obey and you don't want to? It's hard to obey, especially in a world that tells us we should do whatever feels good. Much of the time, obeying doesn't feel good.

We need only look as far as Saint Joseph to see an example of obedience. We don't hear a lot in Scripture about Joseph, but we do know an angel visited him to tell him the truth about Mary's pregnancy and that the message came from God. What must Joseph have thought when he heard that Mary's son, Jesus, would save people from their sins? What does it make *you* think of?

Joseph married Mary even though she was unexpectedly pregnant, and not with his baby. He listened to God and obeyed, even though it meant things would be very, very strange. He might not have known the adventures ahead—the flight to Egypt when King Herod went on a killing spree of the babies in Bethlehem, for example—but he probably suspected it wasn't going to be easy.

That didn't stop Joseph from obeying. He did what God asked of him, even though it was uncomfortable. He said yes to God's will, even though it was going to involve challenges and discomfort.

We shouldn't obey just because it feels good or looks good; we should obey because it's what God asks of us. God has given us authorities in our lives. Let's try to be more like Joseph and obey quickly and completely.

> *When Joseph awoke, he did as the angel of the Lord had commanded him and took his wife into his home.*
> MATTHEW 1:24

 *Jesus, obeying usually isn't very popular. It's also not easy. I need a lot of help to not only obey, but to keep a cheerful attitude as I do it. Please help me. Amen.*

 **Ask Saint Joseph to help you obey today the first time you're asked.**

33

Anticipate

# Friday
## Fourth Week of Advent

**Think**

When I read this passage, I sometimes imagine Elizabeth's feeling the movement of her baby for the first time. I think of her surprise, of how the movement must have felt like a flutter of butterflies, of how she was reminded of her blessings.

For Mary, being the reason Elizabeth felt such joy had to be very exciting and very humbling, a reminder of the important role she had been asked to play. Being the mother of Jesus wasn't going to be easy, but seeing her cousin's happiness must have made her heart soar.

This passage is used in a prayer familiar to many of us, the Hail Mary. Every time we pray the Hail Mary, we can think of Christmas and the joy it brings to the world every year. We're supposed to have the kind of joy Saint John had when he was still inside his mother, Elizabeth: leaping and dancing. We're reminded by this passage that Christmas is close and that we should be ready to exclaim, as Elizabeth did, that the fruit of Mary's womb is born at last!

**Pray**

*Jesus, Saint John knew you even while he was still inside his mother's womb. Help me to know you in my daily life and to have the same joy John and Elizabeth had. Amen.*

**Act**

**Decorate your heart by praying three Hail Marys.**

Anticipate

# Saturday
## Fourth Week of Advent

 We have one more day of waiting. Does it feel like the longest day of the year?

Advent is almost over, and Christmas is tomorrow. But are we ready?

Mary believed what God said before she had any proof. She offered herself and embraced God's will without really knowing what was going to happen. How often do we show that kind of trust in God?

What can we do to make ourselves more like Mary? On this day before Christmas, what small gift can we prepare to give Jesus at his birth? Will it be a good attitude, an act of service, a small sacrifice?

Whether we begin our Christmas celebrations on Christmas Eve or wait until Christmas day, we can hold our hearts wide open for the gift of the Baby who has come for each of us. He brings us the hope of peace and the promise of joy. Let's embrace this gift with all we have and thank God with our whole heart.

*Blessed are you who believed that what was spoken to you by the Lord would be fulfilled.*
**LUKE 1:45**

 *Jesus, I want to be ready for you. Take me as I am, and help me to grow more like you. Amen.*

 **Draw a picture of the Visitation or write a story about it. Share it with your family.**

*Anticipate*

# Rejoice!

*All this
took place to
fulfill what
the Lord had
said through
the prophet:
"Behold,
the virgin shall
be with child
and bear a
son, and they
shall name him
Emmanuel,"
which means
"God is
with us."*
**MATTHEW
1:22–23**

## Think

Finally, it's Christmas, the day we've been waiting for! It's exciting and awesome, isn't it?

Whether you attend Mass on Christmas Eve or on Christmas day, you participate in one of the most important feast days of the Church year. Christmas is one feast that can never be moved or excused: it's *that* important!

Jesus' birth wasn't just about a baby boy being born in a cold stable a few thousand years ago. His birth was part of a bigger picture, a plan God made to fulfill his promise to his people. Jesus was the Messiah, an answer to thousands of years of prayer and waiting.

Each of us is part of something bigger too. God has a plan for our lives, and in the rejoicing we will do today and during this entire Christmas season, we should remember how important that is. God loves us enough to give us a purpose. We don't always know what it is right away, but it's there.

Rejoice! Celebrate Jesus!

36

# Christmas Day

## the CHRIST candle

**Pray**

*Jesus, I'm so happy to finally be celebrating your birthday! Thank you for the gift of your birth and the joy it brings to Earth. Amen.*

**Act**

**Sing! Dance! Give glory to God through your actions.**

At last, our wreath is fully lit. The Light of the World is here! Rejoice! Light the white candle in the center, and as you see the wreath completely lit, pray for the grace to bring this Christmas miracle into every aspect of your life.

*The Octave (eight days) of Christmas begins with the Nativity of the Lord on December 25 and ends with the Solemnity of Mary, Holy Mother of God on January 1.*

# December 26
## Octave of Christmas

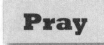

**Think** — Jesus was like many other babies. He was born and wrapped in a blanket to keep him warm. Much of what we read about in Luke's Gospel describes an ordinary birth.

And yet we know Jesus' birth was to become the most special birth ever. The angels announced it to shepherds, a special star heralded his birth, and his mom was a virgin. Not everything was as it seemed; things were far from ordinary.

We do well to remember that Jesus was born poor and, in many ways, forgotten. He wasn't even born in a house; Mary and Joseph couldn't find a room, and Jesus was born in a stable. It was probably cold and drafty and uncomfortable.

To most of the people in Bethlehem, Jesus was just a baby. His birth was no big deal, no cause for concern, no reason to do things any differently.

We might find ourselves taking the same approach. That's why we spend eight days—an octave—celebrating Christmas. Jesus' birth is so important it warrants a season of celebrating.

**Pray** — *Jesus, I need help remembering that Christmas lasts more than one day. Help me remember that the celebration's not over and that Christmas is a season.*

**Act** — **Make a birthday banner for Jesus, and hang it up in your house.**

*While they were there, the time came for her to have her child, and she gave birth to her firstborn son. She wrapped him in swaddling clothes and laid him in a manger, because there was no room for them in the inn.*
LUKE 2:6–7

Rejoice!

# December 27
## Octave of Christmas

**Think** Some things seem too good to be true, and my grandma used to say that when something seems that way, it usually is. Jesus, though, *isn't* too good to be true. He's just what he promised: Messiah and Lord.

Jesus' birth answers a lot of prayers and fulfills the hopes and dreams of many in the ancient world. He does that today too, though we can sometimes get so used to the message of hope and peace that we fail to really hear it.

While the world packs away the Christmas decorations and stores the Christmas music, our celebration is just getting started. We've gotten ourselves ready with Advent, and now we're all set to continue celebrating.

The question, at times, becomes one of *how*. How are we supposed to rejoice and celebrate when everyone else thinks the reason for celebrating is over? What do we do to set this time apart and make it special?

Just as we spent time all through Advent getting our hearts ready for Baby Jesus, we can spend this Christmas season giving our hearts to him. We won't find an actual baby in an actual stable, of course, but he has told us that when we help the weak, the needy, the poor, and the disadvantaged, we help him.

Jesus can be found in the people around us. Let's look closer and share our special Christmas celebration with them.

*For today in the city of David a savior has been born for you who is Messiah and Lord.*
**LUKE 2:11**

**Pray** *Jesus, I want to keep celebrating your birth, but everyone else acts like Christmas is over. Give me ideas and energy to keep my perspective festive. Amen.*

**Act** Share a special dessert or treat with your family in honor of Jesus' birth.

*Rejoice!*

# December 28
## Octave of Christmas

**Think**

Today we have two perspectives to consider. The first is the feast of the Holy Innocents, those babies who were killed when King Herod killed all the boys aged two and under after the Magi left Bethlehem. The second is the rejoicing of the angels in the night sky.

On the one hand, we have to remember that Jesus' birth was not all happiness and ease. Not only was it in a very uncomfortable setting, but because of Herod's jealousy, a lot of other babies were killed.

The sight of the angels in the dark winter sky, lighting it up like day and making a ton of noise, must have startled the shepherds. Many of them were probably dozing. What did they make of this angelic chorus?

The angels give glory to God and mention peace on Earth. This seems to contradict what we know about the death of all those babies.

Things don't always make sense to us. Jesus' dying on a cross many years later on Good Friday didn't make sense to his disciples until that Sunday, when they found the empty tomb and realized the unthinkable had happened: he had risen from the dead!

While we rejoice, let's not forget the sorrow in the world and to remember those less fortunate both in our prayers and in our actions. Let's keep in mind that our rejoicing should lead us back to God and to the many lessons Jesus taught during his life.

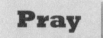

**Pray**

*Jesus, it's hard to imagine the death of all those babies, but it's just as hard to think about a sky full of singing angels. Allow me to have a glimpse of the pain and the joy today as I continue to celebrate your birth. Amen.*

**Act**

**Write a poem or story about someone you love who has died.**

*Rejoice!*

# December 29
## Octave of Christmas

**Think**

Have you ever been so excited you just couldn't hold it in? Have you ever had news to share that made you just want to run and tell the next person you saw? Have you ever just wanted to jump for joy and tell everyone you knew why?

That must be how the shepherds felt after hearing the news the angels brought. I picture them running full-tilt toward Bethlehem, arriving completely out of breath. After the initial shock—a whole host of angels lighting up the sky must have been more than a little startling—they probably wanted to tell everyone they could. The only problem was, they were in the middle of a field, in the middle of the night.

Were the people in Bethlehem annoyed when the shepherds came running into town and shouting so late at night after everyone was in bed? Sometimes we get annoyed when someone else's excitement interrupts us. We might even tell them to be quiet.

The news of Jesus' birth is the most exciting news any of the people at that time had ever heard. It was unbelievable, and the shepherds couldn't hold it in. We should be the same way about it—excited and bursting with joy.

> *When the angels went away from them to heaven, the shepherds said to one another, "Let us go, then, to Bethlehem to see this thing that has taken place, which the Lord has made known to us."*
>
> **LUKE 2:15**

**Pray**

*Jesus, your birth was over 2,000 years ago. Help me to feel your presence and the excitement of your birth today. Amen.*

**Act**

**Read one of the Nativity stories from the Gospels (Matthew 1 and 2 or Luke 1 and 2) with your family.**

*Rejoice!*

# December 30
## Octave of Christmas

**Think** God often picks the most unlikely people to be his messengers. He could have sent the angels directly to the town of Bethlehem, but instead they showed up above a field outside of town to lowly shepherds.

Though we're told the Magi came from a distant land to see Jesus, they came in and out without a lot of fanfare. The shepherds, though, were the bearers of the big news of the Messiah's birth: the world first heard about it from *them*.

As children, it's possible to feel like you're not very important. Sometimes it seems that no one wants to listen to what you have to say. You don't know as much as the older people in your life. You haven't lived through a lot of the experiences you'll need to be an authority.

God can—and will—use you, though. You are just like the shepherds. You can be a bearer of God's Word to the people around you through what you say and do.

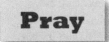

**Pray** *Jesus, I'm just a kid. How can I be important? Help me to see that what I do matters and that I can be your helper. Amen.*

**Act** **Pray for those who are poor and in need of shelter, food, and care. If there is a group in your church or community helping those in need, think of a way you can join their efforts.**

*When they saw this, they made known the message that had been told them about this child. All who heard it were amazed by what had been told them by the shepherds.*
LUKE 2:17–18

*Rejoice!*

# December 31
## Octave of Christmas

 Choosing for his Son to become human is the greatest act of love God could have shown for us.

Being human is not easy. We have a lot of pain and suffering in our lives, and Jesus did too. He was born cold and screaming, barely indoors, with animals. He had a feed box for a bed. Things were far less than clean and sterile in Bethlehem.

The octave of Christmas is almost over, though the Christmas season continues until the Baptism of the Lord, which is usually celebrated the Sunday after Epiphany. We are still in celebration mode. We are still rejoicing over the newborn King.

It's unbelievable that God became a person—not an adult right away, but a baby who would grow up just like us. Think of the hardest parts of being a kid and know that Jesus faced those things too.

Jesus can help each of us in our daily struggles. Even as we rejoice in his birth, we can remember to ask him to be with us in our troubles, however small.

> *And the Word became flesh and made his dwelling among us, and we saw his glory, the glory as of the Father's only Son, full of grace and truth.*
> **JOHN 1:14**

 *Jesus, it's hard to picture you as a young child. I always see you as either a tiny baby with a halo or a grownup surrounded by important people. Help me to find you approachable so I can bring all my troubles to you. Amen.*

 **Bake Christmas cookies and share them with a neighbor or someone who needs extra joy this year. Include a homemade picture or card that will brighten the person's day long after the cookies are gone.**

*Rejoice!*

# January 1

## Solemnity of Mary, Holy Mother of God

 **Think**

It's hard to sit still. It's even harder to sit still and think or reflect. There are so many things we could be doing: games, chores, playing, and so much more.

*And Mary kept all these things, reflecting on them in her heart.*

LUKE 2:19

We have more distractions in our world than ever before. How often do you just turn off everything and sit in silence?

The Holy Spirit is often represented as a still, small voice. God doesn't usually shout to get our attention. He waits patiently and uses the silence.

We need to use Mary's example and spend time in thought. We need to turn off the many things that distract us with noise and opportunities to *do* and let ourselves *be* in God's presence. There's no need to talk, no need to move. Just sit quietly.

It's not easy at first. It's not even very fun at first. But after a while, you might start to savor the time you spend with God in this way.

 **Pray**

*Jesus, there's so much going on all the time around me. Help me to find you by being like your mother and spending time in silence. Amen.*

 **Act**

**Sit in silence for five minutes. Ask Mary to guide you closer to her Son during this quiet time.**

# Feast of Epiphany

**Think**

We don't hear a lot about people "prostrating themselves" before other people. I always picture these kings, in all their fancy clothes, lying flat on the ground before Jesus, who was probably sitting on Mary's lap or on the ground close to her. The floor might have been dirt, and the kings must have been quite a sight.

Then to see the things they brought! They brought gifts fit for a king, though what they saw before them was far different than the usual image of a child king. Jesus was, to all appearances, the child of a carpenter, not wearing the fancy garments or surrounded by the court the kings must have expected.

Even seeing their surroundings, the kings still laid themselves out on the floor at Jesus' feet. They recognized him as a king, even though he didn't look the part.

We're called to do the same. In our everyday lives, Jesus asks us to recognize him in the people around us, to act in a way that shows others that we serve Jesus. The greatest gift we give Jesus is the love we give to the people around us. That's the message of Christmas.

**Pray**

*Jesus, I want to honor you as the Magi did, but I don't have a lot to give. Take my heart and make it yours. Take my actions and bless them so that they glorify you. Take my prayers and help me grow. Amen.*

**Act**

**Draw a picture of the gift you would bring to Baby Jesus.**

> *On entering the house they saw the child with Mary his mother. They prostrated themselves and did him homage. Then they opened their treasures and offered him gifts of gold, frankincense, and myrrh.*
> **MATTHEW 2:11**

# The Story of the Epiphany

At the time  was born, three saw a . The knew that the would lead them to a new king, so the followed the . When they came to Jerusalem, they asked where to find the new king, . told them to go to Bethlehem where the new king would be born, but began to worry. didn't want a new king to take his place. So told the to come back and tell him about . wanted to do

away with . When the  found

, they knelt down and offered

their . That night, God spoke to the

in a dream and told them not to return to ,

so the  went home another way.

---

### Rebus Instructions
Use the key to help with the story.

Jesus

WiseMen

Star

KingHerod

Jesus, Mary,
And Joseph

Gifts

# Rejoice!

**Welcome Baby Jesus** offers daily activities that encourage families to

**Think**  **Pray**  **Act**

based on words from Scripture. These exercises are designed to engage your household during the Advent season by tying Scripture and reflection to your daily life. With each passing Sunday and each candle lighting, your Advent wreath will grow brighter, your family's faith will grow stronger, and the true meaning of this season will be discovered.

In the midst of life on a farm with kids and critters, Catholic wife and mother **Sarah Reinhard** blogs about marriage and motherhood, book talk and rambling remarks, and observations and distractions on SnoringScholar.com.

## Liguori
LIGUORI, MISSOURI

ISBN 978-0-7648-1997-1
50000>

9 780764 819971